America's Leaders

The SECRETARY
of Treasury

by Scott Ingram

BLACKBIRCH®
PRESS

THOMSON
GALE

San Diego • Detroit • New York • San Francisco • Cleveland • New Haven, Conn. • Waterville, Maine • London • Munich

THOMSON

GALE

LIBRARY OF CONGRESS CATALOGING-IN-PUBLICATION DATA

Ingram, Scott (William Scott)
The Secretary of Treasury / by Scott Ingram.
    pv. cm. — (America's leaders)
  Includes index.
Contents: America's chief financial officer — The job of secretary of treasury — Who works with the secretary of treasury? — Where does the secretary of treasury work? - Who can become the secretary of treasury? — A time of crisis — Another time of crisis - A secretary's day — Fascinating facts.
  ISBN 1-56711-283-8
  1. United States. The Secretary of Treasury —Juvenile literature. I. Title. II. Series.

Table of Contents

America's Chief Financial Official

More than 200 years ago, a group of men wrote a document, the U.S. Constitution, which established the American government. The authors of the Constitution divided the government into three separate branches— the legislative branch, the judicial branch, and the executive branch. Under the Constitution, the leader of the executive branch is the president. The president has the power to put laws passed by Congress into effect and to enforce them.

Ever since the first president, George Washington, took office, presidents have had people to advise them. In 1789, the U.S. Congress voted to establish departments in the executive branch to help the president. These were the Departments of State, Treasury, and War. The leader of each department was called a secretary. Together the secretaries formed a group of advisers known as the president's cabinet.

Even before 1789, a department was needed to oversee national financial matters such as taxes and the payment of government expenses. From 1781 until 1789, the states were governed under the Articles of Confederation. The articles established a legislative body known as the Congress of Confederation. The congress established the Board of Treasury to handle national finances.

The Board of Treasury had little actual power, though. Under the confederation form of government, the states were really thirteen separate countries. Some had their own military forces. Each state printed its own money, which had value only within the state's borders. Rhode Island money, for example, could not be used in Virginia. In addition, states were not required to pay taxes to support a national government.

By the mid-1780s, congressional delegates agreed that the confederation of states would collapse without a central government to repay its debts, fund a military, and print a single form of currency.

George Washington was elected the first president of the United States after the Constitution was approved in 1789.

In 1786, 29-year-old Alexander Hamilton, a congressional delegate from New York, requested that all states send delegates to a constitutional convention. The purpose of the convention would be to replace the Articles of Confederation with a governing document that gave a central, national government power over individual states.

Alexander Hamilton was appointed by President Washington to oversee the Department of the Treasury.

Hamilton had served as George Washington's chief military adviser during the American Revolution. Although Hamilton was only in his early twenties during the war, Washington trusted the young officer to obtain and pay the money used for gunpowder, weapons, and other military supplies. Hamilton was widely respected for his service. As a result, when he called for a constitutional convention, other delegates followed his direction. A group of 55 men gathered to create the Constitution in Philadelphia, Pennsylvania.

In 1789, after the Constitution was approved by all states, Washington was elected president. One of his first acts was to give Hamilton the job of overseeing the Department of the Treasury. According to the Constitution, Hamilton, as secretary of the treasury, was "to perform all such services relative to the [nation's] finances as he shall be directed to perform."

The Job of Secretary of the Treasury

Today, more than two centuries after Hamilton, the job of secretary of the treasury is much more complicated than it was in 1789. Yet the requirements of the position are much the same as they have always been.

Treasury Secretary John Snow (left) met with President Bush to discuss financing the war in Iraq in 2003.

The secretary is the chief financial official of the government.

As the chief financial official, the secretary advises the president on the nation's economic progress or problems. He may recommend tax cuts or increases. He may alert the president that certain government policies will increase the debt owed by the country. In 2003, for example, the secretary of the treasury traveled around the United States with the secretary of commerce and the secretary of labor on the "Jobs and Growth Tour." During this trip the secretaries spoke to small gatherings of ordinary Americans. They talked about the ways in which the president's tax cuts could increase jobs and economic growth.

In 2003, the secretary of the treasury (left) traveled around the country with the secretaries of labor and commerce to talk about how tax cuts could help the economy grow.

JOBS and GROWTH

The secretary also has responsibilities that have to do with financial crimes. After the terrorist attacks on the United States in 2001, for example, the Treasury Department investigated banks in the United States in which suspected terrorists may have deposited money. The secretary has the power to hold, or freeze, money in bank if the money could be used to pay for illegal activities.

As the president's chief financial adviser, the secretary is the chairman of president's Economic Policy Council. The council helps to develop the details of overall tax programs the president wants to enact. The secretary also oversees large government programs such as Social Security and Medicare, which provide government funds to retired, elderly, and sick Americans. The secretary also represents the U.S. government in international financial matters. In 2003, for example, the secretary appeared before a meeting of the International Monetary Fund (IMF), a financial organization similar to the United Nations. The secretary requested money from the IMF to help rebuild the war-torn nation of Iraq.

USA FACT

The jobs of the secretary of the treasury and the U.S. treasurer are different. The secretary is the nation's chief financial official. The treasurer oversees the minting of coins and the printing of paper currency. The treasurer reports to the secretary of the treasury.

Treasury Secretary Snow (left) and Federal Reserve Chairman Alan Greenspan met at the Bureau of Engraving and Printing to introduce the new twenty dollar bill in 2003.

Who Works with the Secretary?

Just as the president needs advisers to help run the executive branch, the secretary needs advisers in the Treasury Department. Some advisers work in the office of the secretary of the treasury. The deputy chief of staff handles many of the office's everyday responsibilities when the secretary is away. The chief of staff and deputy chief of staff schedule the secretary's appearances and meetings. The general counsel handles legal matters that affect the office and the secretary.

> **USA FACT**
>
> The Treasury Building was designed in 1833 by Robert Mills, who also designed another capital landmark, the Washington Monument.

In addition to the office staff, the secretary meets with heads of the eleven different departmental offices of the Treasury Department. These people hold titles such as assistant secretary. Most of these offices operate in the Treasury Building.

The secretary also meets away from the Treasury Building with the heads of treasury bureaus, called undersecretaries. These twelve bureaus include the Internal Revenue Service, which handles all tax matters. They also include the Bureau of Printing and Engraving, which handles the production of all paper currency.

Where Does the Secretary Work?

The secretary of the treasury works in the Treasury Building. This structure is the oldest departmental building in Washington. It is also the third-oldest government building after the Capitol and the White House. The secretary's office is on the third floor of the

The Treasury Building is the third oldest government building in Washington, D.C.

five-story building, which covers five acres of ground. Although the building contains 120,000 square feet of space, it has only enough offices for 10 percent of the Treasury Department employees based in Washington.

The White House and Capitol

As a member of the cabinet, the secretary of the treasury meets with the president in the president's main working area, the Oval Office. The secretary also attends weekly meetings with other department secretaries in the White House Cabinet Room. The secretary may also meet at the White House with the president's other closest economic advisers.

The secretary also appears at the U.S. Capitol before members of the Senate and the House of Representatives.

President Bush (center) meets with the department secretaries at the White House every week.

Treasury Secretary Snow met with business leaders around the country in 2003 to talk about the country's economy.

There, the secretary reports on the nation's economic growth and answers questions about the president's economic plan. In the appearances, the secretary may meet with the legislators who work most closely with economic matters and the federal budget. Among these groups are the Senate Finance Committee and the House Ways and Means Committee.

Outside of Washington

The secretary often travels around the United States to meet with leaders of key industries to discuss the overall performance of the U.S. economy. In late 2003, for example, Treasury secretary John W. Snow spoke at business luncheons in several large cities. He reported on

Vice President Al Gore (right) congratulated Larry Summers (2nd left) after he was sworn in as President Clinton's (left) Secretary of the Treasury.

the ways that President George W. Bush's tax and job growth plans had helped the economy. In his speeches, Snow said that the president's plan had created jobs, increased home purchases, and led to a rise in the value of the stock market.

The secretary also travels to foreign countries to build economic cooperation with individual nations or with groups of nations that are in the same region, such as in Europe, Africa, or Asia. In this role, a secretary might discuss monetary exchange rates. The value of a U.S. dollar in foreign currency—peso, yen, euro, or other forms of money—changes frequently. The secretary must work with financial leaders of other countries to maintain fair exchange rates.

Who Can Become Secretary of the Treasury?

Although Alexander Hamilton was a lawyer, most people who have served as secretary of the treasury have had backgrounds in business and industry. Because they are responsible for overseeing the president's economic plans, secretaries support the economic programs of the president.

> **USA FACT**
>
> The oath of office taken by the secretary of the treasury is written in the Constitution. It is the same oath taken by the president, vice president, and all the members of Congress. It states:
>
> *I do solemnly swear (or affirm) that I will faithfully execute the Office of (the appropriate office), and will to the best of my ability, preserve, protect and defend the Constitution of the United States.*

Like other members of the cabinet, the secretary of the treasury is nominated by the president. The nominee must appear before the Senate Finance Committee. This group of 21 senators interviews the nominee. After the interview, the committee votes on whether to send the nomination to the full Senate.

If the committee approves the nominee, the full Senate then votes. A nominee who receives a majority vote, more than 50 of the total of 100 senators voting in favor, is approved. Once the nominee is approved, he or she is sworn in. The secretary is traditionally sworn in at the Treasury Building.

A Time of Crisis

The first secretary of the treasury, Alexander Hamilton, faced serious financial problems when he took office in 1789. The biggest problem was the national debt. In all, the states owed more than $75 million to foreign countries and to American citizens who had loaned money to support the colonial military during the Revolution. Because states had operated almost independently before the Constitution, some states owed large debts and some owed very little.

When Alexander Hamilton became treasury secretary, the national debt was seventy five million dollars.

Hamilton felt that it was critical for the United States to build a good financial reputation with other nations as well as with all its citizens. To do this, he believed, the federal government had to assume (pay) the debts of every state by passing a tax that all states would pay.

Wealthy states, such as Virginia, strongly objected to Hamilton's plan. That state had already paid its debt. State leaders did not want to pay again to wipe out the debts of poorer states such as South Carolina and Rhode Island.

Congress, especially lawmakers from Virginia, opposed Hamilton's plan and created a crisis that threatened the financial health of the new country. Hamilton solved the problem with the Compromise of 1790. In return for the Virginia lawmakers' agreement to support the federal debt repayment plan, the capital of the nation would be relocated from Philadelphia, Pennsylvania. Hamilton agreed to legislation for a new capital that would be built along the Potomac River near the border of Maryland and Virginia. The new city, called Washington, D.C., became the capital in 1800.

USA FACT

The assassination of President William McKinley in 1901 led many Americans to call for a nonmilitary government force to protect the president. At the time, the only such force in existence was the Secret Service. In 1902, at the request of Congress, the Secret Service assumed the responsibility of protecting the president.

Another Time of Crisis

Salmon P. Chase (1861–1864) was the secretary of the treasury under Abraham Lincoln when the Civil War began. The war caused an immediate need for more government money, so Chase created the Internal Revenue Service, which taxed citizens for the first time. At the time, however, a good deal of the money coming into the treasury in taxes was worthless. The loose banking laws of the time allowed state banks—more than 1,600 in all—to design and print their own paper currency. Many of the bills resembled federal bills, but they were counterfeit, or fake.

Salmon Chase created the Internal Revenue Service to raise money for the government by taxing citizens.

By 1863, almost half of the money in circulation in the United States was counterfeit. The government had no way to prevent counter-feiters from passing worthless bills into circulation. As a result, Chase persuaded Lincoln to establish a federal law enforcement unit separate from the military. This force would track down the source of counterfeit money and arrest anyone who printed or distributed it. Lincoln was assassinated before the unit could be established. In July 1865, however, President Andrew Johnson and Congress acted on Chase's recommendation and created the Secret Service to fight counterfeiting.

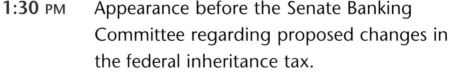

A Secretary's Day

The secretary of the treasury is a busy person whose days are filled with meetings, press conferences, and speeches, both in Washington and in other cities or countries. Here is what a day might be like for the secretary of the treasury.

6:00 AM   Wake, shower, read overnight changes in dollar to yuan exchange rates from China.

7:00 AM   At work in Treasury Building; meet with chief of staff to preview schedule.

8:30 AM   Meeting at White House with president's economic policy council to discuss tax cuts.

10:30 AM   Return to Treasury Building to meet with Japanese finance minister on tax policies toward U.S. businesses operating in Japan.

12:00 PM   Luncheon speech on the president's energy plan and its benefits for the economy at annual meeting of the Center for Energy and Economic Development.

1:30 PM   Appearance before the Senate Banking Committee regarding proposed changes in the federal inheritance tax.

4:00 PM Press conference at Treasury Building on the new steps being taken to protect money that workers have invested to use after retirement.

6:00 PM Dinner with business leaders from nations of the European Union.

10:00 PM Briefing from general counsel about upcoming trip to meeting of foreign finance ministers of the International Monetary Fund.

As chief financial officer of the U.S. government, the secretary of the treasury spends long days in meetings and press conferences on the nation's many economic issues.

Fascinating Facts

Alexander Hamilton, the first secretary of the treasury (1789–1795), was killed in a pistol duel in 1804 with Aaron Burr, who was at that time the vice president.

Albert Gallatin

Albert Gallatin (1801–1814), who served the longest term as secretary, was born in Geneva, Switzerland. He was asked to serve as an officer in the Hessian forces, German soldiers who fought for the British in the Revolution. Instead, he fled to the United States in 1779.

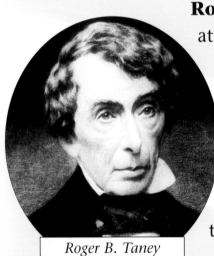

Roger B. Taney

Roger B. Taney (1833–1834) served as attorney general before becoming secretary. He served as chief justice of the Supreme Court after leaving the treasury position.

Salmon P. Chase (1861–1864) served as the chief justice of the Supreme Court after leaving the treasury position.

Thomas Ewing who served as treasury secretary in 1841, was named the first secretary of the interior in 1857. He was the father-in-law of the famous Union general William T. Sherman.

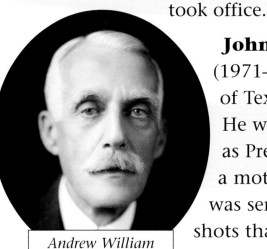

Thomas Ewing

Andrew William Mellon (1921–1932) was one the three wealthiest men in America when he took office.

John B. Connally (1971–1972) was the governor of Texas in November 1963. He was riding in the same car as President John Kennedy in a motorcade in Dallas and was seriously wounded by the shots that killed the president.

Andrew William Mellon

Secretaries 1789–2003

Alexander Hamilton 1789–1795

Oliver Wolcott, Jr. 1795–1800

Samuel Dexter 1801

Albert Gallatin 1801–1814

George Washington Campbell 1814

Alexander J. Dallas 1814–1816

William Harris Crawford 1816–1825

Richard Rush 1825–1829

Samuel D. Ingham 1829–1831

Louis McLane

Louis McLane 1831–1833

William John Duane 1833

Roger B. Taney 1833–1834

Levi Woodbury 1834–1841

Thomas Ewing 1841

Walter Forward 1841–1843

John C. Spencer 1843–1844

George Mortimer Bibb 1844–1845

Robert John Walker 1845–1849

*William Harris
Crawford*

William Morris Meredith 1849–1850

Thomas Corwin 1850–1853

James Guthrie 1853–1857

Howell Cobb 1857–1860

Philip Francis Thomas 1860–1861

John Adams Dix 1861

Salmon P. Chase 1861–1864

William Pitt Fessenden 1864–1865

Hugh McCulloch 1865–1869

George S. Boutwell 1869–1873

William Windom

William Adams Richardson

1873–1874

Benjamin H. Bristow 1874–1876

Lot M. Morrill 1876–1877

John Sherman 1877–1881

William Windom 1881

Charles J. Folger 1881–1884

Walter Q. Gresham 1884

Hugh McCulloch 1884–1885

George S. Boutwell

Daniel Manning 1885–1887

Charles S. Fairchild 1887–1889

William Windom 1889–1891

Charles Foster 1891–1898

John G. Carlisle 1893–1897

Lyman J. Gage 1897–1902

Leslie M. Shaw 1902–1907

George Bruce Cortelyou 1907–1909

Franklin MacVeagh 1909–1913

William G. McAdoo 1913–1918

Henry H. Fowler

Carter Glass 1918–1920

David Franklin Houston 1920–1921

Andrew William Mellon 1921–1932

Ogden L. Mills 1932–1933

William H. Woodin 1933

Henry Morgenthau Jr. 1934–1945

Fred M. Vinson 1945–1946

John Wesley Snyder 1946–1953

George Magoffin Humphrey

1953–1957

Charles Foster

Robert Bernard Anderson 1957–1961

C. Douglas Dillon 1961–1965

Henry H. Fowler 1965–1968

Joseph W. Barr 1968–1969

David M. Kennedy 1969–1971

John B. Connally 1971–1972

George P. Shultz 1972–1974

William Edward Simon 1974–1977

W. Michael Blumenthal 1977–1979

George William Miller 1979–1981

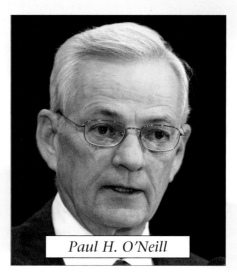
Paul H. O'Neill

Donald Thomas Regan 1981–1985

James A. Baker III 1985–1988

Nicholas F. Brady 1989–1993

Lloyd M. Bentsen 1993–1994

Robert E. Rubin 1995–1999

Lawrence H. Summers 1999–2001

Paul H. O'Neill 2001–2003

John W. Snow 2003–

James A. Baker III

Glossary

adviser—a person who works closely with another person and provides them with information and suggestions

cabinet—a council of presidential advisers

Congress—the legislative branch of the government, composed of the House of Representatives and the Senate

Constitution—the document that established the U.S. government and that contains the principles of the nation

currency—paper money

economy—a nation's system of making, transporting, and selling products and services

exchange rate—the difference in value between currencies of different nations

financial—having to do with money and banking for a government or large organization

House Ways and Means Committee—a group of forty-three congressional representatives who review all budget matters for the federal government, also known as the Committee on Means and Ways

nominee—a person who has been proposed to fill a certain position

Oval Office—the office in the west wing of the White House from which the president works and meets with advisers

Senate Finance Committee—a group of twenty-one senators who interview nominees for secretary of the treasury

tax—an amount of money citizens are charged by governments for general public benefit

The president works and meets with the members of the cabinet in the Oval Office at the White House.

For More Information

Books

Feinberg, Barbara. *Cabinet.* New York: Twenty-First Century, 1997.

Jones, Veda. *Alexander Hamilton: First U.S. Secretary of the Treasury.* Bridgewater, NJ: Bt Bound, 2002.

Wellman, Sam. *The Cabinet.* Minneapolis: Chelsea House, 2001.

Web Sites

United States Department of the Treasury
www.ustreas.gov/index.html
The home page of one of the best general Web sites for the details of a government department.

U.S. Treasury Kids' Page
www.ustreas.gov/kids
Fascinating facts about the treasury for young people.

Education: Duties and Functions

www.ustreas.gov/education/duties/index.html
A detailed explanation of the entire Treasury Department.

The Treasury Historical Association

www.treasuryhistoricalassn.org
A site with a monthly newsletter that includes background on the department and a history of the Treasury Building.

Federal Reserve Bank of San Franciso

www.frbsf.org/federalreserve/money/funfacts.html#A2
A site with interesting historical information about money throughout U.S. history.

Index